G000090734

7 Life Lessons from Noah's Ark

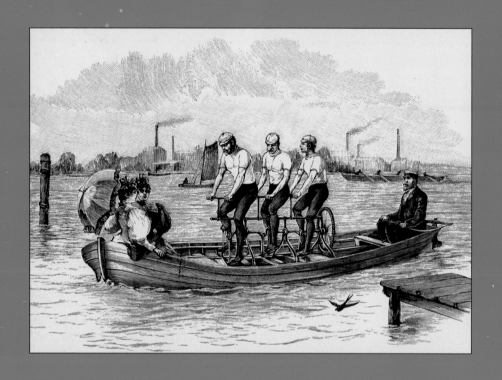

7 Life Lessons from Noah's Ark

How to Survive
A Flood
in Your Own Life

Michael Levine

Celestial Arts
Berkeley | Toronto

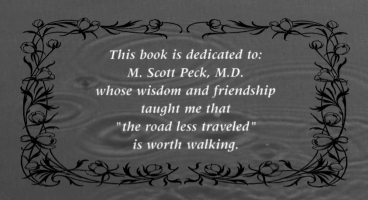

This book is dedicated to:
M. Scott Peck, M.D.
whose wisdom and friendship
taught me that
"the road less traveled"
is worth walking.

Celestial Arts Publishing
A Division of Ten Speed Press
PO Box 7123
Berkeley CA 94707
www.tenspeed.com

Celestial Arts titles are distributed in Canada by Ten
Speed Canada, in the United Kingdom and Europe by
Airlift Books, in South Africa by Real Books, in Australia
by Simon & Schuster Australia, and in New Zealand by
Southern Publishers Group.

Cover & text design by Brad Greene / Greene Design
Photography by Photo.com
Line art courtesy of Dover Publications
and San Francisco Public Library

ISBN 1-58761-200-3

Library of Congress Cataloging-in-Publication Data available from the publisher.

Printed in Singapore

1 2 3 4 5 6 7 / 09 08 07 06 05 04 03

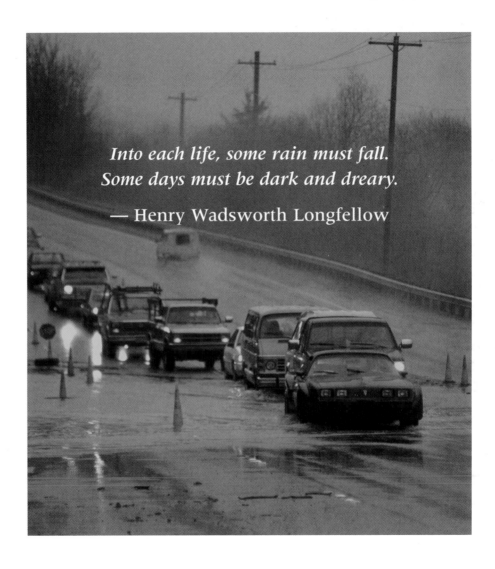

Into each life, some rain must fall.
Some days must be dark and dreary.

— Henry Wadsworth Longfellow

Acknowledgements

My journey from a less than ideal childhood to Hollywood success to writing this book was an unusual blessing and a divine journey filled with people, who for reasons I still do not fully understand, chose to support and encourage me when that was not always easy. To each, my deepest appreciation.

My office staff, Paul Armstrong, Clarissa Clarke, Phil Foord, Dawn Miller, and Amanda Wasvary, who work tirelessly to perform extraordinary miracles. Each of you has my real respect.

My longtime friends, whose never-ending loyalty and belief in me made Life, when it was challenging, worth fighting for. Peter Bart, Adam Christing, Richard Impressia, John McKillop, and Cable Neuhaus.

Special thanks to my friend, David Marlowe, for his extraordinary assistance and spiritual guidance on this work.

And, to the team of Brad Greene, the exceptional designer of these pages, and Veronica Randall, a remarkably gifted woman, editor, friend, and mentor, who helped bring life to this work.

What's Inside

In the Beginning...

Foreword

The Bible is a very, very old book that a whole lot of people take very, very seriously. It has been printed in every language that exists and can be found on every continent, in every country, in every corner of our planet. It is the most widely read, the most thoroughly studied, and **the most consistently argued about work of all time.**

As you probably already know, the Bible is composed of two Testaments, the Old and the New, which are each in turn divided into more easily digestible chapters and more readily quotable verses. The Old Testament is sacred for Jews; the entire text, both Old and New Testaments, is sacred to Christians; and both are also highly important and influential for the billion or so followers of Islam. Theoretically, anyone belonging to one of these three great religions is expected to live their life according to the Bible's teachings. **Easy enough if you're a saint.**

The Old Testament bristles with a prodigious assortment of historical adventures, ranging from the momentous Big-Bang creation of the universe to the endless trials, tests, and tribulations of the men and women who inhabit its tumultuous narrative.

The star of the Old Testament is an omniscient, omnipotent, omnipresent God who is by turns generous, just, and loving with a seemingly limitless array of miracles at his fingertips. But He is also an uncompromising taskmaster who does not hesitate

Big-Bang

creation of the universe

to mete out punishment with breathtaking creativity.

His revenge against those who displease Him takes many forms, including but not limited to plagues, pestilence, and ferociously bad weather.

Perhaps the most challenging aspect of the Old Testament is that more than half of it is chock full of laws that inhibit or prohibit believers from doing just about anything that might have to do with, well, having . . . fun.

The list of **Things You Cannot Do,** of activities and practices that are strictly forbidden in the books of Leviticus and Deuteronomy alone include promiscuity, covetousness, eating pork chops, working on the Sabbath, and getting a hair cut.

For most of us, emulating a righteous lifestyle is no longer as practical as it once was, say several thousand years ago. Many of the Bible's teachings seem old fashioned, even anachronistic in today's world. And yet on any given Saturday or Sunday, more people in America attend synagogue and church services than all the fans combined who crowd themselves into stadiums over the course of a month to watch sporting events. If nothing else, this suggests **there's still a whole lot of Faith being felt out there.**

Finding relevance and applicability to our lives with just one story from the Old Testament is the challenge of this little book. Most of us still have an immediate and obvious identification with many of its stories, and the most well-loved of these is the story of Noah and his ark.

8

THE STORY OF
NOAH

If we did all the things we are capable of doing,
we would literally astound ourselves.

—Thomas Alva Edison

We think we know Noah's story pretty well, don't
we? Very old, very *righteous* man is simply minding
his own business, when he gets singled out to save
not only himself and his immediate family, but also
the future of all humanity. Plus, he must collect and
harbor a representative sampling of the world's

birds and beasts and bugs before a forthcoming deluge the Almighty One plans to unleash that will blanket the entire planet and wipe out each and every inhabitant who dwells upon it. Whew!

One can only imagine Noah's dumbfounded response when he comes face to face with God who complains that **He is sick of all the sin He sees** and thus intends to destroy the very folks He took the trouble to create in the first place.

"I shall wipe out men and women, whom I have created, from the face of the earth, for I am grieved that I have made them, for the earth is filled with violence because of them."

Noah was the only man on the entire planet in whom God found favor. So He instructed the pious patriarch to build a vessel that would remain afloat throughout the forthcoming deluge for an unprecedented forty days and forty nights; and all this, mind you, to be accomplished long before blueprints, building permits, or Home Depot.

"Make yourself an ark of cypress wood, make rooms in it, and coat it with pitch. This is how you are to build it: The ark is to be 450 feet long, 75 feet wide, and 45 feet high. Put a door on the side, a window on top, and build three floors: a lower, a middle, and an upper deck. I am going to bring floodwaters on the earth to destroy all the life I have created under the heavens, every creature that has the breath of life in it. Everything on earth will perish. But I will establish my covenant with you, and you will enter the ark, you and your sons and your wife and your sons' wives with you.

"You are to bring into the ark two of every living creature, male and female, to keep them alive with you. Two of every kind of bird, of every kind of animal, and of every kind of creature that moves along the ground will come to you to be kept alive. You are to take every kind of food that is be eaten and store it away for you and for them."

After his up-close-and-personal encounter with the Almighty, Noah abandoned his chores, his flocks, and his fields and constructed a sea-worthy structure on the approximate scale of your average football stadium. He even did his best to warn his neighbors of the impending catastrophe. But those who heard him scoffed and snickered, treating him less like a divine prophet and more like a wild-eyed lunatic.

But Noah steadfastly embraced his mission— with a zeal that was a glowing testament to **the enduring vitality of his Faith.**

And lo, these many millennia later, about the only thing upon which both scholars and scientists can agree, is that accepting this (or any other account

from the Bible, for that matter) as a literal recon-
struction of what actually occurred can best be
seen as a matter of our Faith.

In their 1999 book, *Noah's Flood: The New
Scientific Discoveries About the Event That Changed
History,* geologists Dr. William B.F. Ryan and Dr.
Walter C. Pitman of Columbia's Lamont-Doherty Earth
Observatory conducted an expedition throughout
the region that today is Turkey. They found artifacts
and took soil samples that helped advance the
long-held idea that a gargantuan deluge of water
from the Mediterranean, rushing through the
Bosporus with the force of twenty Victoria Falls,
entered the Black Sea some 7,600 years ago. In a
little under two years, they theorized, the Black Sea
rose and inundated the surrounding plains,
demolishing everything in its path and altering the

landscape, until it arrived at its present dimensions.

Ryan and Pitman suggest that people living in the region fled, dispersing south, east, and even up into northern Europe, and that this astonishing upheaval became part of the collective folk memory. Refugees from the Black Sea flood carried the experience with them into the Levant. In time, this legend gave rise to the Babylonian flood myth found in the ancient epic of Gilgamesh and, later, the saga of saturation segued from local lore to the Biblical tale of Noah.

Great flood stories are by no means exclusive to the peoples of the Middle East. There are, in fact, *hundreds* of flood myths and ark legends found worldwide, including the Chinese, the ancient Hawaiian, Native American, New Zealand's Maori and Australia's Aboriginal cultures.

However, the task of separating myth from reality, legend from lore, facts from fiction, is not the point. Authenticating or disproving the Noah experience, or any part of his fantastic voyage, is for others to argue.

Noah was clearly ambitious. He was certainly devoted. And he was most definitely obedient. Additionally, he and his sons may have also been more than just a little meticulous, because the ark wasn't seaworthy for nearly a hundred years.

When God announced the floodwaters were ready to be loosed upon the earth, as commanded, **Noah loaded all the creatures aboard, as tradition has so long held, two by two.**

When Noah and his family entered the massive vessel, it was God, Himself, who sealed the ark, and

two by two

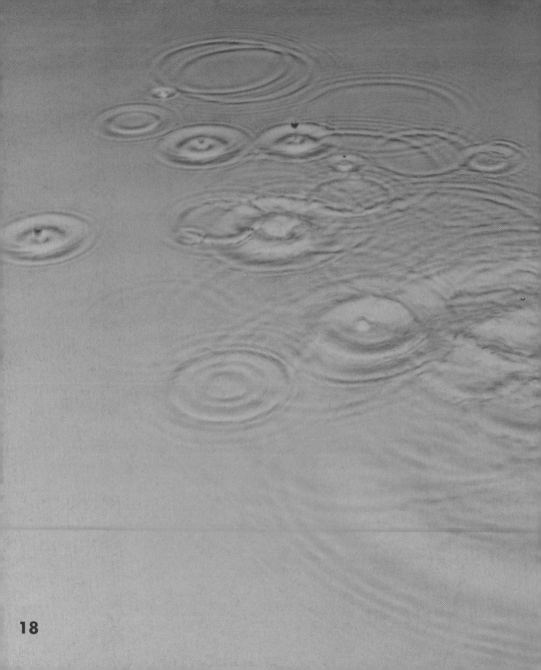

18

said, "Seven days from now I will send rain on the earth for forty days and forty nights, and I shall wipe from the face of the earth every living creature I have made."

On the seventeenth day of the second month, right on schedule, the rain began to fall and fall and fall. The floodwaters lifted the ark high above what was once the ground, and the ark rose and rose and rose still more as water covered the trees, and then the hills, and finally the mountain tops.

Every living thing on the earth that was not tucked away safely inside the ark perished. Kapoot.

Finally, the rains stopped falling and God sent a great wind over the earth and the waters slowly, slowly receded.

On the seventeenth day of the seventh month, the ark came to rest on the mountains of Ararat in Turkey.

After another forty days, Noah opened a window and released a raven into the cloudy sky. The black bird flew and flew until, finding no place on which to land, it returned to the ark. Seven days later, Noah sent out a dove. But the dove could find no place to rest because there was still nothing but water covering the earth. So she, too, returned to the ark.

Seven more days passed and again Noah sent the dove from the ark. When the dove flew back to him, there was in its beak a freshly plucked olive leaf—the first sign that the waters had begun to recede from the earth.

Noah waited seven more days and then again sent forth the dove.

This time she did not return to him.

Then God said to Noah, "Come out of the ark, you and your wife and your sons and their wives. Bring out every living creature that is with you—the birds, the animals, and all the creatures that move along the ground—so they can multiply on the earth and be fruitful and increase their numbers upon it.

"Never again will I curse the ground because of man, even though every inclination of his heart is evil from childhood. And never again will I destroy all living creatures as I have done."

Then God blessed Noah and his sons, saying to them, "Be fruitful and increase in number and fill the earth. All the animals, the birds, the fish are given into your hands. Everything that lives and moves will be food for you. Just as I gave you the green plants, I now give you...*everything*."

And then God said, "This is the sign of the covenant I am making between you and every living creature, a covenant for all generations to come. **I have set my rainbow in the clouds, and it will be a sign of the covenant between the Earth and Me.**"

Just what, you may well ask, does all this Biblical **condemnation and redemption** have to do with us?

Simply this: Whether or not you believe Noah's odyssey to be fact or fable, gossamer or gospel, legendary legerdemain or lyrical lunacy, his legacy offers much, much more than a how-to for building and launching a floating zoo long before power tools, air conditioning, and indoor plumbing. Much, much more.

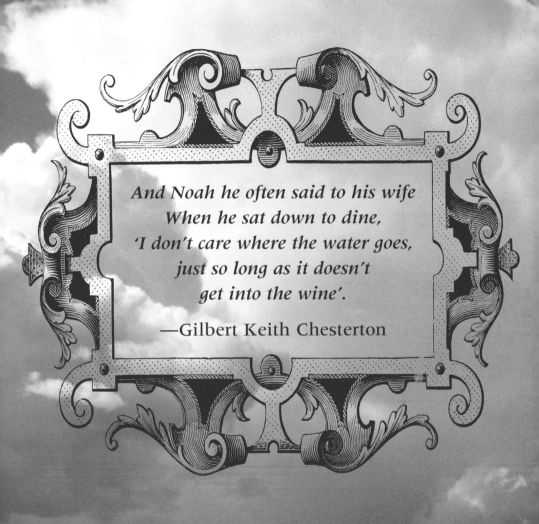

And Noah he often said to his wife
When he sat down to dine,
'I don't care where the water goes,
just so long as it doesn't
get into the wine'.

—Gilbert Keith Chesterton

Chapter 1

Don't Miss The Boat:
The Lesson of Opportunity

Out of clutter, find simplicity.
From discord, find harmony.
In the middle of difficulty, lies opportunity.

—Albert Einstein

I'm sure we can all agree that Opportunity is never a lengthy visitor, in fact, it is often downright fleeting. The elements that come together to create any new enterprise, whether grand or modest, are in constant flux; so the **liquid circumstances** that make up an Opportunity one moment may well be radically altered or even evaporate altogether by the next. Therefore, we must be prepared, willing, and available to seize Opportunity the moment it comes calling.

So we need to keep everything open—our eyes, our ears, our minds, and our hearts—to the potential for Opportunity. Naturally, it would help to recognize one when we see it. And it isn't always obvious. Some opportunities look like, well, nothing much. While others look like, um, the end of the world. If this sounds vaguely familiar it's because our friend Noah's big Opportunity WAS the end of the world. While his friends and neighbors caroused and cavorted in all sorts of unseemly ways, Noah took control of his own destiny. Oh, and the future of all humankind as well. Not to mention the fate of every other living species on the planet. Very Big Stuff.

"So how does this relate to me and to my life?"

you may well ask. Because it isn't enough to simply recognize an Opportunity; it is also most imperative that we act on it. AT ONCE! That's how.

Grabbing an Opportunity means being willing to take Action. Being willing to take action means being willing to take a Risk. Being willing to take a risk means being willing to embrace Change.

Thus, **Opportunity = Action + Risk = Change.**

But the thing about change is, very rarely is it a welcome guest in our midst. Change is the stranger in town. The **elephant in the room.** Change is never familiar, seldom cozy, often uncomfortable, and usually at least a little bit scary. That's why we resist it, of course. Because we don't see Change as the exhilarating new prospect it could be, the exciting portent of

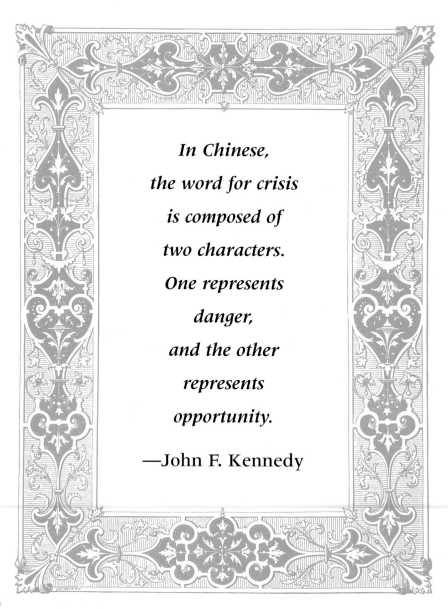

*In Chinese,
the word for crisis
is composed of
two characters.
One represents
danger,
and the other
represents
opportunity.*

—John F. Kennedy

limitless potential it should be. We're a bit wary, rather cautious, a little suspicious. Opportunity so often looks more like disaster, calamity, and crisis. Because we don't recognize it for what It Is.

So, we must be willing to adjust our perception of what is a catastrophe and what is an Opportunity. Or, put another way, is this Opportunity a catastrophe in the making? Or is this catastrophe an Opportunity in disguise?

Thus we come face to face with the Unknown. And that's scary. Isn't it? Or is it? Well, sure it is . . . IF YOU AREN'T CRAZY! Not only is it absolutely, positively **normal to be afraid,** it would be rather worrisome if, when confronted with the Opportunity to risk everything, you weren't just a teeny bit nervous. Change, by it's very nature, carries with it the possibility of failure. And fear of

failure, oddly enough, is what keeps us Safe.

Safe from failure because we didn't risk anything.

See, that's the thing about risk, my friends. Taking a risk means not knowing the outcome. Risky ventures don't always work out the way we expect them to, want them to, or hope they will. That's what makes them risky. See?

Taking a risk could just be a big fat waste of time, or energy, or money, or emotion, or _____ (you fill in the blank).

But, if you don't take the chance, reach for the opportunity, seize the moment, the outcome is ALWAYS the same: **nothing.**

no risk + no change = no NOTHING

Nothing happens. You're home safe.

Safe from new people, places, and things; like new relationships, new environments, new lifestyle choices, new career opportunties _____ (you fill in the blank).

Yup. You're safe all right. Or are you?

Well there's no doubt about it, staying put is much comfier than moving on. It requires less effort, for one thing. Radical change always requires some effort. And it almost always requires a radical shift in thought or behavior or both. Usually both. It nearly always requires us to Do something. Or do Something. Often both.

So you can't be lazy or passive or complacent AND take advantage of the opportunties that— lucky you—have come your way. Sorry. It doesn't work that way. It's takes work. Hard work to make your luck work for you.

Another great seafarer, Christopher Columbus, was surely not the first to dream of a shortcut along

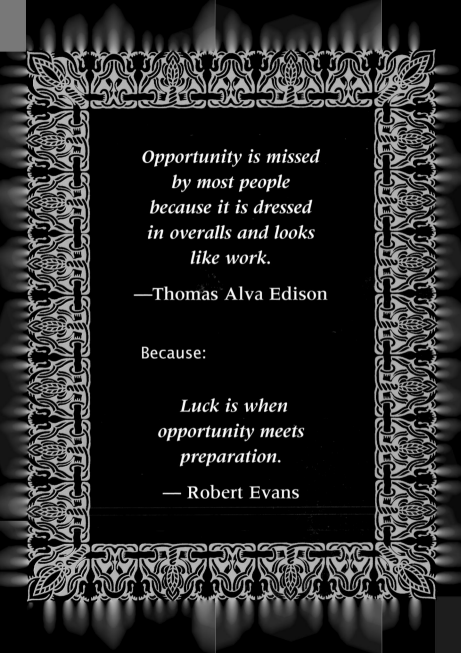

*Opportunity is missed
by most people
because it is dressed
in overalls and looks
like work.*

—Thomas Alva Edison

Because:

*Luck is when
opportunity meets
preparation.*

— Robert Evans

the trade route to the Indies and traversing the far reaches of the unexplored ocean; he was simply the first to dream it AND attempt it. His historic adventure was nothing less than the most ambitious and daring enterprise of the century (or possibly any century). In order to carry it off he had to ignore the universally accepted notion of the day, **namely that his ships would plummet off the face of the earth once they sailed over the edge of the visible horizon.**

By facing and even embracing the paralyzing fear and overwhelming doubt of the unknown, Columbus was able to go where no European had gone before. He didn't allow the seemingly impossible odds to stop him before he started. He didn't wait for the safe bet, the sure thing, the easy path, because he knew there wasn't one. By refusing to accept the acceptable limitations of his time, he flew, or rather sailed, in the face of popular belief in order to seize his moment. And with meticulous planning, heroic effort, and a wide-open mind—he sailed all the way to a new world. And, by the way, he didn't arrive where he expected to, wanted to, or hoped he would. And the rest is history. Do you see where I'm going with this?

Here's where I'm going: Going someplace new or trying something different is never really a waste of time or effort because, here's the good news—YOU REALLY CAN'T LOSE!

"The optimist sees opportunity in every danger; the pessimist sees danger in every opportunity. A pessimist sees the difficulty in every opportunity; an optimist sees the opportunity in every difficulty."

—Sir Winston Churchill

See?

If you stay open to the outcome (despite your own expectations or the expectations of others) whatever it may be, how can you possibly lose?

And this is where **Faith** comes into it.

If you put your Faith in: the dream, the project, the journey _____ (you fill in the blank), and you do whatever it takes to:

_____ (you fill in the blank), and stay open to whatever the outcome may be; _____ (you fill in the blank), the Opportunity will ALWAYS pay off.

NO MATTER WHAT. I promise. You'll see. Keep reading.

Chapter Two

We're All in the Same Boat: The Lesson of Community

We must learn to live together as brothers or perish as fools.

—Martin Luther King, Jr.

Sure, it may seem obvious, but it also happens to be true. No matter how great the contrast we think there is between us, either collectively or individually, whether our differences arise from gender, race, nationality, geography, culture, education, employment, politics, philosophy, religion, or our hair-dos: We're All in the Same Boat.

Let me say this again. No matter how **odd, strange, bizarre,** or **exotic** our neighbors may appear to us (or we appear to them), no matter what language they speak, what they eat, what they wear, what they drive, or what they live in—they are the same as us. We are all Homo Sapiens, members of the same family, **just plain folk** sharing the same lonely planet as it hurtles through the solar system.

Earth is, as far as we know, the only friendly outpost in the inhospitable vastness of outer space, so the concept of a global Community clinging to its crust is not only practical, it is essential. Especially when you consider the alternative. Which is Isolation.

And Isolation + Division + Destruction = Death.

If these statements seem obvious—they should be. But the uncomfortable truth is they make some folks, well, uncomfortable. Maybe they make you

EARTH

uncomfortable. If so, ever asked yourself why? If not, let's ask it now. Why does the stuff that makes us different from each other divide us from each other?

Well, mostly because the stuff that makes us different is, well, **different.** Different in the sense of unfamiliar. And that which is unfamiliar to us is unfamiliar usually because we

a) have little or no experience with it and, thus, we

b) don't understand it, and what we don't under-
    stand we

c) tend to be suspicious of, and if we're suspicious we

d) aren't likely to accept it, and if we don't accept it,
    how can we

e) respect and coexist with it?

And therein lies the problem: lack of acceptance as a result of (a not unreasonable) wariness because of (a perfectly understandable) lack of understanding thanks to (an entirely forgivable) lack of experience.

Trouble is, this can lead to (a dangerously and unfortunately rather common) isolationist position: "I simply won't acknowledge what I don't respect/accept/trust/understand/recognize."

I think you'll agree that **Isolation** is hardly the key ingredient in the recipe for a strong sense of Community. And (I repeat), Community is pretty much all we have. Am I harping? Well, just wait, you'll soon see why.

The thing is, we ARE different from one another in ways too numerous to describe in a book of only 152 pages. We look, sound, smell, work, play, quarrel, kiss, behave, and believe differently—okay, I've admitted it. But **despite appearances,**

we really are more fundamentally alike than we are diverse.

From birth we all share the basic needs for food, water, protection from the elements, and social interaction. Without them we die of malnutrition, dehydration, exposure and isolation, respectively. The most interesting of these to me is isolation. Why? Because a human infant can receive adequate requirements of nourishment and shelter and still die if she is deprived of physical contact with her kind. That's right. If a baby isn't touched, held, cuddled, and cooed at—he'll just die.

This is why solitary confinement is so effective. Because unless you are a male orangutan, you will eventually **go mad** if you are denied human contact. Am I making my point about Community?

Never doubt that a small group of
thoughtful and committed citizens
can change the world. Indeed, it is the only
thing that ever has.

—Margaret Mead

The point, in case it's still hazy for you, is that we may just have to come to terms with respecting and accepting those whom we don't really understand and aren't experienced with. A tall order, I know. But, again, not so insurmountable when you examine the alternative: **Isolation + Division + Destruction = Death.** Remember?

Where does respect for others come from when it comes without the benefit of understanding? Where does acceptance come from when it comes without the guarantee of familiarity? They come

And where does this sense of Community come from, exactly? How do we achieve it? Well, for a start, practice makes perfect.

⚓ Each time we welcome a stranger into our midst we reject Isolation.

⚓ Each time we visit a new place without fear of getting lost we dismiss Division.

⚓ Each time we embrace a new idea without needing to agree with it we avoid Destruction.

⚓ Each time we give our time and attention to someone or something without expectation of a reward we banish Death.

from a sense of Community. Which is the recognition that we're all in it together.

Each and every time. Sounds like a global Community is indeed a saner, safer, less scary, and even more navigable place to live, doesn't it?

But wouldn't Earth be an exceedingly drab little world without a little variety? Absolutely. Isn't that why the Almighty gave Noah the heads-up in the first place? So the smorgasbord of species He had already gone to the trouble of creating would be preserved for the less liquid future? You bet.

So let's also be absolutely clear that, while a sense of Community calls for a collective sense of wholeness, by no means does it suggest that we discard the many differences among us, the very things that distinguish us as us. By no means. The trick is to figure out a way to **celebrate**

our differences, not deny that they exist.

If we were willing to consider all the things that would normally separate us from one another and acknowledge and accept them—not adopt, just accept—as being okay—different, but just fine—I suspect we'd be well on the way toward a peaceful but lively coexistence.

And on the ark, we know the lion had to lie down with the lamb. (Well, maybe not WITH the lamb. Maybe they were on different decks.) But cohabitate, they did. For forty days and nights.

If the story of Noah teaches us anything it is that a Cooperative Spirit of Community Had to Prevail. Or what? Well, a lot of critters would have been left behind to drown in the downpour, that's what. The hippos shared quarters with horses who shared with hares. The gibbons and the geese bunked with the gnus. The pythons had to promise not to swallow the pigs. The dogs had to leave the cats alone, and the cats had lay off the rats. Even the spiders had to swear off the flies.

This is **Faith** at the Community level. Even with seemingly irreconcilable differences amongst them, even without perfect understanding or previous experience of one another, respect and acceptance huddled together in the same boat— and all were spared—even the flies.

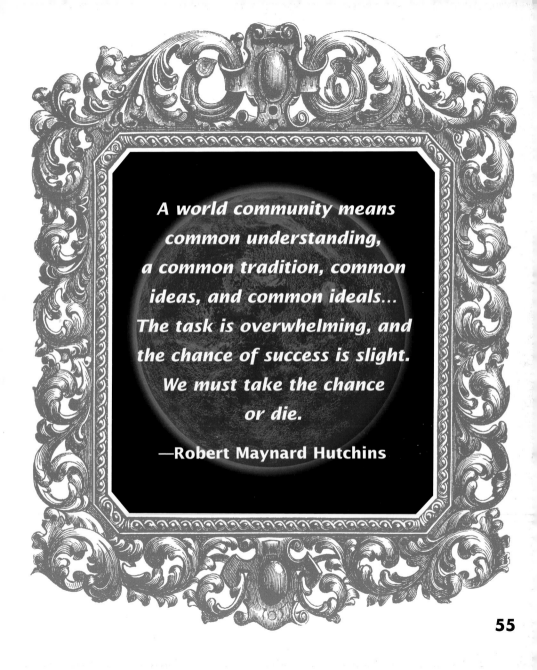

A *world community means common understanding, a common tradition, common ideas, and common ideals... The task is overwhelming, and the chance of success is slight. We must take the chance or die.*

—Robert Maynard Hutchins

Chapter Three

Stay Shipshape: The Lesson of Healthy Balance

Give me health and a day and I will make the pomp of emperors ridiculous.

—Ralph Waldo Emerson

Balance—what is it exactly? It is exactly the equilibrium of two opposing forces. Like energy versus inertia. Discipline versus chaos. Hedonism versus asceticism. Too much versus not enough.

We know we're supposed to want Balance in our lives because we've been told a thousand million times, and because we know that creating

Balance in life is healthier than living in a state of **extremes**—don't we? Or do we? Well, in an overindulgent consumer culture like ours, wanting a balanced life is one thing—sustaining a balanced life is quite another.

First of all, why is Balance better? Well, it's usually cheaper for one thing.

Let's look at just one example: It takes neither an MD nor a CPA to recognize that the stress-reducing, mood-elevating endorphins we get with low-cost (often free) aerobic exercise not only lift us out of depression rather quickly, they are a far more cost-effective (often free) alternative to antidepressants, and without those undesirable side effects. Like reduced desire, for one thing. I'm talking about sexual dysfunction folks—a primary side effect of anti-depressant medications. (Ironic, isn't it? That an

*anti*depressant would cause a really *depressing* symptom like reduced desire? No thanks.)

Also, overindulgence with food, legal recreational drugs (oh, like alcohol and cigarettes) and illegal recreational drugs (you know which ones I mean) can really put a strain on your bank Balance—in more ways than one. Because not only do luxuries like these come at a price, they overburden your body as well. Which means potentially more doctor/hospital/specialist visits, possibly more prescription medications, perhaps even higher insurance rates, (let's not even discuss rehab/detox/therapy programs) and so on. Thus, overdoing it can have repercussions that are physically as well as financially taxing.

But wait, there's more. About a zillion studies have shown that staying in good physical condition

in turn affects your emotional well-being. So unless you've been out of the country for a very long time, you know that maintaining a program of regular physical activity—be it jogging, swimming, skiing, bicycling, bowling, ballroom dancing, figure skating, lifting weights, climbing mountains, shooting baskets, vaulting poles, walking dogs, hitting tennis balls, base balls, golf balls, or gardening—is better for your head and your heart than sitting on your fanny. **Unless you are reading.**

And, who knows, **maybe you'll even have more sex.** Heck, you'll be in better shape, so you'll look, feel, and be more attractive. Far from tiring you out, exercising is actually energizing. Staying physically active remains the closest thing we have found thus far to a fountain of youth. That's why they're called recreational

No man ever repented that he arrived
from the table sober, healthful, and
with his wits still about him.

—Jeremy Taylor

activities (in case you wondered) because they literally recreate us. In other words, maintaining good health is the most surefire way we have to slow the rate at which we die.

However, it is imperative to recognize that staying mentally and physically fit requires that you get a move on even when you don't feel like it. Wait till you're in the mood, and you'll never make it off the couch. Rome wasn't built in a day, and neither were you. You cannot simply erase a lifetime of overindulgence overnight, no matter what the diet and exercise industries may claim! It takes time and consistency and patience—and did I mention realistic goals?

Sensible expectations will mean the difference between an extreme New Year's resolution that is doomed to failure:

"Starting January 1st I will drop 30 pounds in 30 days."

And a slowly progressive and ultimately permanent shift in lifestyle:

"Starting today I will steadily increase my _____ (you fill in the blank) and gradually cut back on my _____ (you fill in the blank).

Healthy Balance also means routinely indulging in moderation and really splurging every once in a while. Enjoying a glass of red wine with dinner will not only enhance the atmosphere at the table, the medical community now agrees it helps the circulation of red blood cells. That first cup of coffee in the morning really does expand the sleepy blood vessels in your brain and stimulate your memory. And why not polish off a big wedge of pizza or pie a la mode on a special occasion? Not with every meal, but every now and then. In other words: Enjoy your life. Please. Just do it in a balanced way.

Too much of anything is generally not a good thing. Too much dieting or too much exercising can be just as debilitating as too much eating or drinking. Balance. Remember? It's the same principle as: All work and no play not only makes Jack a dull boy, it could kill him. Balance.

So, Balance requires a long-term, that is to say, a lifelong commitment. **Commitment to yourself. For life.** If that sounds a little selfish—it is. And your life depends on it. It is also rather selfless. How so? Because others are depending on you.

What's good for you is also potentially beneficial for those around you, those who rely on you. Like your spouse, your children, your friends, your employer, your employees, your colleagues, your customers, your clients, your patrons, your parents, your students—all the people who need you, your

skills, your talent, your taste, your perspective, your energy, your example, your generosity, your leadership, your love. Let me say it again: What's good for you is good for them.

So taking care of yourself is not just about you. It's also about caring for others who count on you to take care of them.

That's why ships are always, well, shipshape: You take care of the vessel that is going to take care of you. Simple, isn't it? It just makes sense to put your **Faith** in something you've taken good care of. Doesn't it? Tending to the needs of your body, mind, family, home, job, community, country is a Balancing Act—no question. So start small. Start with yourself. Because without you, the rest doesn't matter anyway.

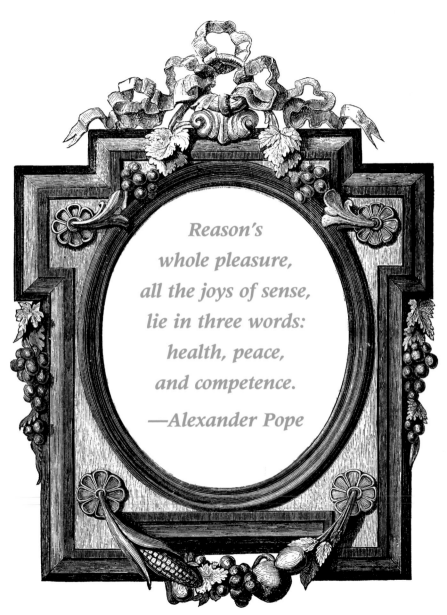

Reason's
whole pleasure,
all the joys of sense,
lie in three words:
health, peace,
and competence.

—Alexander Pope

71

Chapter Four

Don't Give Up the Ship:
The Lesson of Perseverance

No matter what will be said and done,
preserve your calm immovably;
and to every obstacle, oppose patience,
perseverance, and soothing language.

—Thomas Jefferson

This is an easy one. Well, sort of. It's pretty much a
case of: When the going gets tough the tough get
going. Get it? Whether you want to fly jets or join
the circus or re-tile the bathroom or save France,
there comes a moment in every life when you must
stop listening to the critics and nay-sayers all

around you, have the courage of your own convictions, and simply get on with the job.

History is littered with anonymous characters whose job it is to discourage, dissuade, and disdain anyone from doing much of anything new or different, anything that might upset the status quo. You probably know some folks like this. I've got two words for you: **Don't Listen.** Interesting, isn't it, that the names we remember and celebrate are those that flew—sometimes literally—in the face of convention and did what they thought, what they believed, what they knew they had to do. You probably know some folks like this. I've got two words for you: **Pay Attention.**

> *There is nothing like a dream*
> *to create the future.*
>
> —Victor Hugo

Remember our friend Christopher Columbus who was nearly laughed out of Spain when he proposed a new route to the East Indies—by sea? Forget shlepping overland across the Hindu Kush along the dry and dusty Silk Road to Cathay, Burma, and the Spice Islands. His dream, and more importantly, his **Perseverance in pursuit of his dream,** changed the course of history.

And with a little Perseverance, or maybe a lot, the pursuit of your dreams could do the same. Think about that for a moment.

The closest friends of Alexander Graham Bell begged him to see reason and drop the hopelessly futile project that was consuming all his time and attention, not to mention cash. They eagerly encouraged him to turn his clever brain and considerable talents to other, more worthwhile, more lucrative endeavors. This farfetched notion of transmitting audible speech through electrical wires was sure to drive him straight into bankruptcy, to say nothing of shredding his professional reputation. When Bell became immensely famous, and immensely wealthy thanks to his improbable invention, he got even with his "friends" by refusing to grant them even a few shares of company stock when he incorporated Bell Telephone. Proving yet again there's no revenge quite like success, is there? But that's another book.

The Wright's were encouraged by family and friends to load up on life insurance before launching their ambitions and themselves into their flimsy flying contraption and possibly plunging into personal and financial ruin. This was a dream that virtually no one, save the brothers themselves,

thought would ever get off the ground, either literally or figuratively.

I could clutter the remaining pages of this book with exhaustive examples of the heroic explorers and prophetic inventors, the iconoclastic artists and pioneering scientists, the maverick military leaders and muck-raking political activists that have left us **dazzled in jaw-dropping wonder** at their dedication, their courage, and their foresight over the centuries—but I won't. Instead, I'd like to focus on what these famous folks have in common, namely, their Focus.

> *Genius,*
> *that power which dazzles mortal eyes,*
> *is oft but perseverance in disguise.*

—Henry Willard Austin

Where do the visionaries get their gumption? For starters, they keep their eyes on the prize. That is, they keep their Focus on the objective in front of them. They deflect the **zinging slings and arrows of dissent and damnation** with total concentration on the task at hand.

This is what allows them to keep a Commitment. Without the ability to Focus, making a Commitment becomes, well, iffy, if not altogether moot. And Commitment is another common denominator among the highly accomplished. Commitment to a cause, to a place, to a person, to an idea, to an ideal—the list is endless—and really only possible with Perseverance.

Because committing to something or someplace or

someone is not easy. Hardly ever. Almost never. That's why it requires a Commitment in the first place. Because it's probably hard. And making a Commitment is pointless without Follow-Through.

The leaders and movers and shakers and discoverers throughout our history have Follow-Through in spades. This is why they've become household names. Because they Followed Through. Thus,

Perseverance = Focus + Commitment + Follow–Through

"How," you may be asking right about now, "does this apply to my life?" After all, you may not be after a Pulitzer or be in contention for a berth on the Olympic team. You may not aspire to making history, nor wish to alter the course of human events. But here's the thing. You do, no matter what you do. Everything you begin and end has an impact on something. **Everything you do and say counts.** Everything you Focus on, Commit to, and Follow Through with makes a difference. Everything. Please remember this.

So, future Nobel Laureate or not, do not think for a minute that whatever you're doing RIGHT NOW is trivial, or doesn't matter. It isn't, and it does.

And if you believe in it, whatever it is, then KEEP DOING IT. With your whole heart. This is **Faith.** Persevering no matter what. Persevering despite popular opinion, despite the accepted wisdom of the past, despite the obstacles thrown in your path, despite the indignities of fear and loneliness. Do it anyway, despite all this.

And so, despite judgement and ridicule from virtually everyone in the known world, Noah did not allow his attention on his God-given assignment to wander for even a moment. For a hundred years he chopped and pounded and spread pitch until the ark was finished. A hundred years. That's a long time to Persevere, in case you were wondering. And how easily his discipline and determination could have been undermined by all the sneering and jeering from his neighbors. But his Faith in God's promise did not waver. **Faith** that was judged by others as the mere folly of a delusional old man.

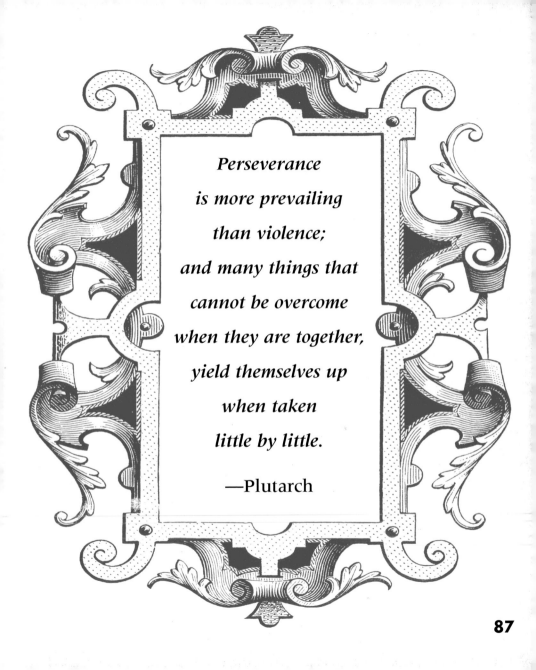

*Perseverance
is more prevailing
than violence;
and many things that
cannot be overcome
when they are together,
yield themselves up
when taken
little by little.*

—Plutarch

Chapter Five

Stay True to Your Course: The Lesson of Character

Character isn't inherited.
One builds it daily by the way one thinks and
acts, thought by thought, action by action.

—Helen Gahagan Douglas

It comes down to this for me: More and more, in fact, as often as possible I prefer to conduct my daily life, professional and personal, work and play, with people whom I've come to trust and respect and who trust and respect me. Wouldn't we all prefer that? Wouldn't you?

Sure you would. Isn't it a lot less stressful to do business with people you know aren't going to cheat you or take advantage of you? Isn't a lot more relaxing to hang out with people you know aren't gossiping about you the instant you leave the room? Of course it is. Are YOU that kind of person? Would YOU like to be your colleague? Would YOU like to be your friend? Look in the mirror. Who do you see?

Do the eyes that meet your gaze sparkle with courage, consideration, and compassion? In short— do they shine with Character? And what is that, exactly? What is this slightly nebulous catch-all con-cept called Character?

It may be easier to find the answer by asking a different question: How do you acquire good Character? The answer is, you can't. Sorry.

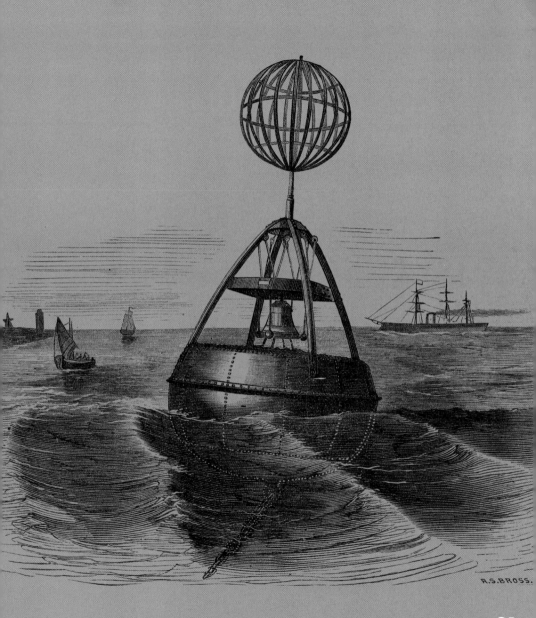

R.S.BROSS.

Character ain't for sale. Character is earned. Little by little, day by day. You don't GET it. You DO it.

Like what? Well, like taking Responsibility for stuff. What's so hard about that? After all, who doesn't want to be in control? Except that it's not the same thing. Not at all. Control only gives you **temporary authority** over persons or events. Responsibility gives you **permanent power** over yourself and what goes on around you. Which would you rather have? If you selected the latter, this is called destiny. Imagine, calling the shots on your destiny?

But if you take Responsibility, don't you also run the risk of taking the blame for everything? Absolutely—unless you have Accountability. Accountability serves to remind you that

everything you do and say counts. And it should, because it does. Everything. Remember?

But if you are Accountable for everything, isn't that the ultimate loss of control? You bet it is—unless you have Self-Control. Use it and You Will Do the Right Thing Every Time. Every single time. So:

Character = Responsibility + Accountability + Self-Control

See, the thing about control—it's not about having carte blanche to do whatever you want. It's about choices. And if you have choices, you have freedom.

Exercising your freedom to choose, whether those choices impact the world or just your waistline, is the ultimate test of your Character. So next

time you exercise your freedom to choose where you want to eat out tonight, or who you want for President, or how you want to acknowledge an acquaintance, or if you want to sleep with your girlfriend, or when you're going to discipline your child, remember this: You are making yourself who you are with every decision you make or put off, with every thing you say or keep quiet about, with every thing you do or choose avoid doing.

So that's the Big Secret: Character is not about personality—it's about behavior. Character is not about what you're like, it's about who you are. Character embodies the concept that What You Do *is* Who You Are. And each situation you find yourself in is another opportunity to add to your Character.

Because your character is You.

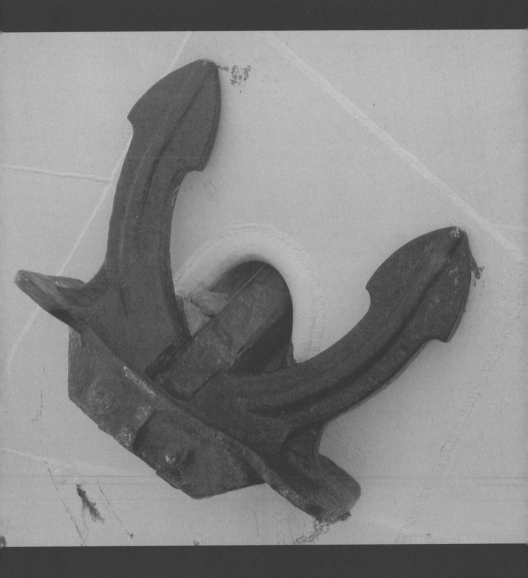

And what goes around comes around. Right? So if you want the surly waiter at that pricey bistro to treat you with a little less attitude and a lot better service, then you must be courteous toward him—first and unfailingly—no matter what. Get it? Then see what happens.

What people say behind your back is your standing in the community.

—Edgar Watson Howe

For better *and* worse, like it or not, what people say about you when you're not in the room—doesn't matter if it's the boardroom, the classroom, or the bedroom—is a pretty clear indication of how you are perceived. So if you want the dish on you to be sweet not sour, you'd better act accordingly.

You see, trustworthiness, generosity, honesty, and respect from others comes mostly from being trustworthy, generous, honest, and respectful towards others yourself. **It starts with you.** Not them.

So if you wish whoever dinged your car in the parking lot this morning had had the integrity to leave a name and number on your windshield, first ask yourself how forthcoming you'd be in the same situation? Would you own up and risk a hassle plus higher insurance rates? Or slink away? **It starts with you.** See? So before you start whining about how little there is to count on in the world, first ask yourself, "Who can count on me?" Can you count on you? Are you willing to be Responsible for your words and deeds? Are you willing to be Accountable for your choices and decisions? Are you

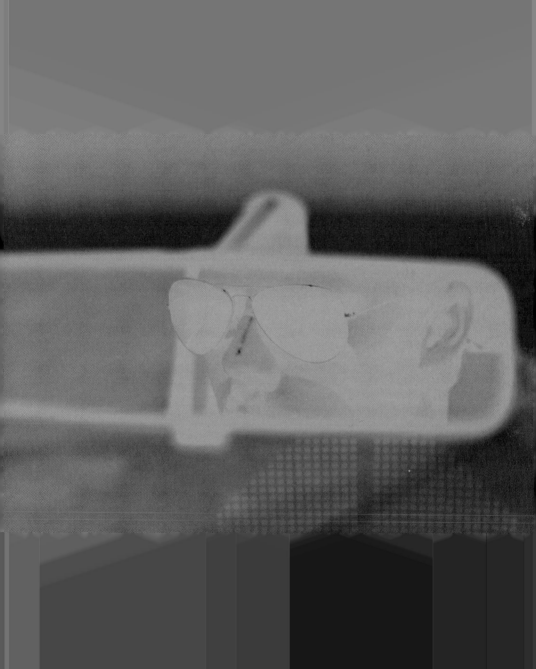

willing to indulge in some Self-Control instead of self-indulgence? Are you willing to *own* your own Character?

Lest we forget, the Almighty One placed the Destiny of all of Creation in Noah's hands. Why, when he was already an old man, was he charged with carrying out a nearly impossible series of tasks? Because God Himself could count on our venerable friend.

Now go back to the mirror for another look. Is the person looking back at you someone you want to know? Is he someone you can count on? Is she someone you have Faith in? Are you someone in whom others can put their **Faith?**

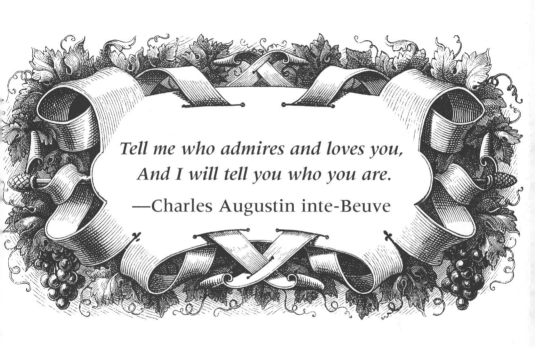

Tell me who admires and loves you,
And I will tell you who you are.

—Charles Augustin inte-Beuve

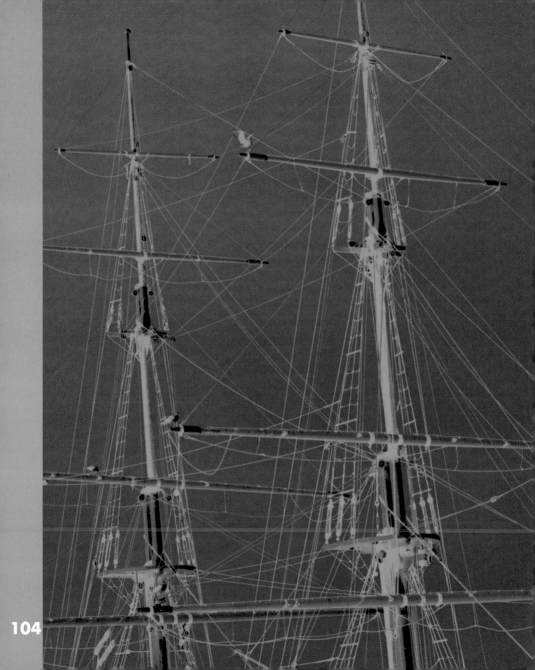

Chapter Six

The View from The Crow's Nest: The Lesson of Perspective

If you look at what you have in life,
you'll always have more.
If you look at what you don't have,
you'll never have enough.

—Oprah Winfrey

Some people have suggested that the ability to put things into Perspective is a God-given gift. Nonsense. **It's a gift you give yourself.** Changing and gaining Perspective can be as simple, or as complicated, as a shift in

Point of View. Sometimes the shift is a radical one; sometimes a very subtle change is all it takes. Whether it's slight or stupendous, being able to spot and study a problem from another angle and then objectively assess the situation is a skill that can be learned and honed, just like needlepoint or navigation or Norwegian. But there are a few requirements, a few steps you must take to get you there.

The first step is Letting Go. Let's say someone ordered you to build a really big boat and you have no clue where to begin because you've lived in the desert all your life. What to do? After you freak out, scroll down the list of "reasons" why you can't possibly do this job: You've been quite happily growing grapes and tending goats and don't want to change careers in mid-life; you know you're wife and kids are going to throw a fit about relocating; you know

nothing about nautical construction. Once you've

catalogued you're "issues," let 'em go. Just chuck

them out the window (or through the tent flap).

Perspective is nothing short of liberating because it

frees you from the "interference" of the past.

Releasing the ghosts of past

experience like fear, pain, anger, shame,

envy, ignorance, bitterness, prejudice, and failure

will lighten your emotional load and bring you

closer to a point of clear-headed objectivity. Which

is the point.

Next, look at your predicament from a different

Point of View. Is this really a messy debacle waiting

to happen? Or is it a compelling Opportunity in the

making? While the challenges will be formidable, no

question, there's always the flip side of the coin.

Let's see, you'll be learning tons of new practical

skills, oh yeah, and you and you're loved ones will actually get to live. Hmmm. . . .

Now let's look at it from someone else's Point of View, like maybe someone who doesn't get to come aboard. Hmmm. . . . How are things looking now? An alternative Point of View really snaps things into focus, doesn't it?

Now you're ready for the Big Overview. Ever wonder why the explorers and pioneers always moved to higher ground to scan the horizon or kept watch from high up in the crow's nest? To give them a broader Perspective on the Earth spread before them. **It literally pushes back the horizon and expands the world.** Imagine. By sizing up the scene from a higher vantage point the limits of their vision at ground or sea level were removed. In the same way,

When the doors
of perception are
cleansed, things
will appear as
they truly are.

—William Blake

raising your vantage point and lifting your Perspective can remove the restrictions you impose on yourself and reveal the multitude of options open to you. Thus, you can in effect push back your horizon and expand your world. Imagine.

But sometimes letting go of what you know is a little too scary. And it is certainly possible to get too many points of view, too much input in the interests of making the best-informed decision possible. And there are times when the view from above encompasses way more than you hoped for and becomes more confusing than clarifying. We all suffer from the daily effects of **data smog,** the on-rushing tidal wave of chronic communication, a little of it vital, a lot of it vapid, some of it sacred and most of it profane: five hundred television channels, all-news radio, newspapers, magazines, the internet, e-mail, regular mail, junk mail, voicemail, videophones, faxes. Can any sane person, in a 24-hour Earth day, keep up with it all? I think not.

We're all so busy, busy, busy just trying to survive our own lives, it's easy to forget that each day actually adds up to a whole life. Mine. And yours. So sometimes it's best just to calm down, take a few deep breaths, stop trying to steer, and simply float a while.

The very act of doing nothing at all, taking no action, can, under the circumstances, be the wisest course of action. Take a decision-making sabbatical (comes from the word Sabbath, in case you hadn't guessed). Biblically speaking, we should honor God's Commandment to rest once a week in any event. So, relax. Step back. Chill out. **And just enjoy**

the view from wherever you are.

Believe me, I know when you're up to your neck in alligators it's hard to remember to appreciate the beauties of the swamp. But see, that's Perspective. It reminds us that the alligators belong in the swamp, just as much as the orchids and water lilies do.

When Noah was ordered to do the impossible by the Almighty Himself, Perspective made the impossible possible. And when he found himself adrift in a raging tempest, he did just that—he drifted. He didn't struggle or try to steer, he just let the ark ascend with the rising waters.

Perspective is the closest we will hope to come to the Divine Omniscience of God. And this is why it is so valuable a gift. Perspective helps us cope

with uncertainty. It helps us manage the chaos around us. It helps us make sense of unfairness and make peace with violence. It helps us love the unlovable and forgive the unforgivable. **Perspective, in a sense, makes Faith in the unfathomable possible,** because it gives us the equanimity to so.

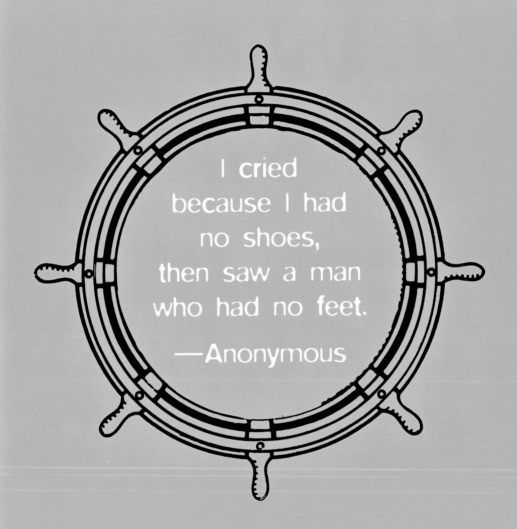

I cried
because I had
no shoes,
then saw a man
who had no feet.

—Anonymous

Chapter Seven

Sink? or Swim? The Lesson of Good Judgement

The opposite of love is not hate,
it's indifference.
The opposite of faith is not heresy,
it's indifference.
The opposite of life is not death,
it's indifference.

—Elie Weisel

Decision, decisions, decisions. You make them all day, every day, a thousand times a day. The Judgement calls you make add up to the sum of your life.

Relinquish those choices to others and you relinquish your life. Finally, hopefully, the whole of your life will be greater than the sum of its parts. At least, that's what I think about and hope for when I think about and hope for Enlightenment.

Of course, you know making the right call, or taking the sensible course, or doing the decent thing doesn't necessarily mean making the obvious, or easy, or popular choice. Using Good Judgement is often difficult, sometimes lonesome, and seldom glamorous. It can be a complicated business, which is why it's, well, helpful to have some help along the way.

And there's a lot of help out there. Maybe a little too much. For starters, we educate ourselves practically from the cradle through college. Twenty years

and sometimes more to learn a whole lot of stuff.
Fascinating stuff, for sure. But
useful? I'm not so sure. The halls of academia team
with brilliant minds that have split atoms and meas-
ured the universe. But who among them can calcu-
late the depth of a dog walker's wisdom or the
breadth of a cab diver's soul?

> *A wise man is nothing more than*
> *a fool with a good memory.*
>
> —Ryan Moore

There are also those who have made careers from
helping others. Therapists, psychologists, psychia-
trists. They keep us company as we reveal ourselves
to ourselves. And we need it. The company, I mean.
Self-revelation can be a tedious and tiring process,

When a wise man points at the moon, the imbecile examines the finger.

—*Buddha*

and most of us need a little coaching, and a lot of encouragement to keep going.

Then, there is the self-help industry: a self-sustaining juggernaut that includes books, audiotapes, videotapes, television shows, radio call-in shows, workshops, and seminars. Self-sustaining because **the more it "helps" the more help we seem to need.** Yup, there's lots of help out there.

And lastly, but certainly not least, there are our religious institutions. No lack of variety there. Whatever you're preference or penchant: Liberally conservative? Conservatively liberal? Fundamentalist? Or totally out there? There's a denomination to serve you. Indeed, religious freedom is our right and one that most of us hold very dear.

Religion in organized form was designed to summon order out of chaos. It gives us, among other things, codes of behavior, that is, **rules to live by.** And these come in darned handy when circumstances change, or get frustrating, or become frightening. In short, all the great religious teachings have sought to guide the believer toward making sound, moral decisions.

So here we are back at Good Judgement. In fact, dear reader, that's pretty much what this modest little book has been about all along: Good Judgement. I don't mean judging other people, like your boyfriend, or your boss, or your next-door neighbor, or your personal assistant, or your yoga instructor, or the guy who just cut you off on the freeway. They *are not* for you to judge. Period. I do mean using Good Judgement about yourself, about **what you're doing in the world, why you're doing it, and how you're doing it.**

These *are* for you and you alone to judge. Period.

Good Judgement is not something we can afford to take for granted. (I certainly can't.) With it, we Swim. Without it, we Sink. It rarely comes quickly or easily. But we can get better at it. Like everything else, it takes intention and practice. No matter what situations we face or under what circumstances we face them, Good Judgement requires that we:

⚓ recognize Opportunity so we Don't Miss the Boat,

⚓ have a sense of Community by accepting that We're All in the Same Boat,

⚓ maintain the benefits of Healthy Balance by Staying Shipshape,

⚓ vow Perseverance and Don't Give up the Ship,

⚓ remember our Character by Staying True to Our Course,

⚓ and get some Perspective with a View from the Crow's Nest.

Sorry, no shortcuts. And no safe harbors either. The right thing to do isn't always the safe thing to do. But that's why we have Faith. Faith in our ourselves. **Faith** that we can and will Survive the Floods in Our Lives.

And that's why the Lord thought that we, His creation, were worth saving in the first place. If He didn't, then Noah and family would have gone to a watery grave along with the rest. And you and I with them. But God, my friends, had Faith in Us. And so we're here today, wondering why we're here.

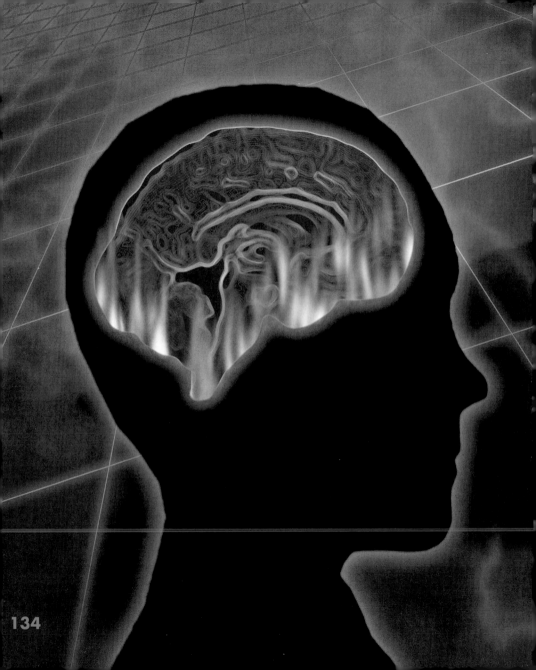

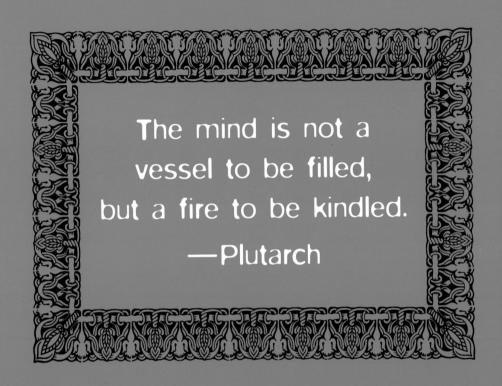

The mind is not a vessel to be filled, but a fire to be kindled.

—Plutarch

Rainbow's End:
The Lesson of Redemption

Look upon the rainbow,
and praise Him that made it.

—The Apocrypha XLIV, II

A rainbow is nothing more, and nothing less, than an arc of sunlight formed when its rays are refracted and reflected by rain drops, or the spray from a waterfall, or mist, or fog. Tradition suggests that a rainbow is comprised of the primary colors red, blue, and yellow and the secondary colors orange, green, and violet. In fact, a rainbow is a continuum of colors, ranging from red to violet, including a host of hues the eye cannot even see. The "bow" refers to the group of nearly circular arcs of color surrounding a common center.

Rainbows are relatively rare occurrences since, in order to see one, both precipitation and sunshine must share the same space in the sky at the same time. To this day, the sight of one still astonishes us. It tells us the storm has passed, the worst is over, that it's safe to venture forth and go on with business of living.

And this was the rainbow's message to Noah: The storm had finally passed, the worst was indeed over, and eventually it would be safe to go out and begin again.

Against the odds, Noah had done all that the Lord had commanded: The ark took a hundred years

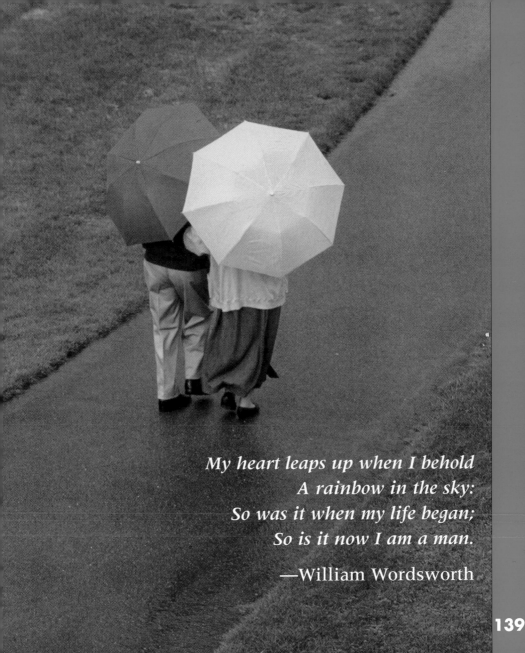

My heart leaps up when I behold
A rainbow in the sky:
So was it when my life began;
So is it now I am a man.

—William Wordsworth

to build (no power tools, no Home Depot, remember?). A male and female of every bird and bug and beast living on Earth was collected and loaded into the hold. All manner of foodstuffs to feed the voracious horde through dark days and darker nights was grown, harvested, and stowed. Finally, Noah and his household went aboard and sealed themselves inside.

For more than a month the rains and tides swept over the ark, lifting the Lord's lifeboat high above the land. The storm ceased at last, and the flood waters receded, and after endless, aimless floating the ark finally went aground on a mountain peak— and guess what? It wasn't the end. It was only the beginning . . .

ABOUT THE AUTHOR

Michael Levine has written thirteen books, including *Lessons at the Halfway Point, The Princess and the Package, Selling Goodness, Take It From Me,* as well as *Guerrilla P.R.,* which is the most widely-used introduction to Public Relations in the world.

Mr. Levine's essays have appeared in *The New York Times, The Los Angeles Times, Reader's Digest, The Hollywood Reporter, The San Francisco Chronicle, U.S.A. Today,* among many others.

His weekly column, *Entertainment Today,* is circulated throughout Southern California.

Michael Levine is also the founder and owner of Levine Communications Office, one of the most successful entertainment Public Relations firms in the country.

www.levinepr.com

Bibliography

The Archaeological Encyclopedia of the Holy Land (3rd Edition). Abraham Negev, ed. Old Tappan, NJ: Prentice Hall, 1991.

The Ark of Noah. David Fasold. Wynwood Press, New York, 1989.

"The Ark-shaped Formation in the Tendurek Mountains of Eastern Turkey," *Creation Research Science Quarterly* 3:1976.

The Bible as History. Werner Keller. New York, NY: Bantam, 1974.

Biblical Archaeology. American School of Oriental Research. Baltimore, MD: Johns Hopkins University Press.

The Catholic Encyclopedia, Volume 1. Robert Appleton Company.

Challenge: Torah Views on Science and Its Problems (2nd Edition). Aryeh Carmell and Cyril Domb, eds. New York, NY: Feldheim Publishers, 1988.

"The Date of Noah's Flood—Literary and Archaeological Evidence." David Livingston. *Bible and Spade,* 6/1: 13-17, 1983.

Discovered: Noah's Ark. Ron Wyatt. Nashville, TN: World Bible Society, 1989.

"The Flood and Noah's Ark." Andre Parrot. *Studies in Biblical Archeology No. 1,* The Philosophical Library, New York, NY: 1955.

The Harper Atlas of the Bible, James B. Pritchard, ed. Science News Books, 1988.

"The Impossible Voyage of Noah's Ark." *Creation/Evolution.* Robert A. Moore. Issue #11, 1983.

The Interpreter's Dictionary of the Bible. Nashville, TN: Abingdon Press, 1976.

Lying: Moral Choice in Public and Private Life. Sissela Bok. New York, NY: Vintage Books, 1978.

Noah: The Personal Story in History and Tradition, University of South Carolina Press, 1989.

The Noahide Society's Ark-Update, David Fasold. Issue No.5 Jan/Feb, 1992.

"Noah's Ark?" William Shea. *Bible and Spade* 1/1: 6-14, 1988.

"Noah's Ark?" William H. Shea. *Archaeology and Biblical Research,* Volume 1 (1) 1988.

"Noah's Ark: Its Final Birth." Bill Crouse. *Bible and Spade 5:3,* 1992.

Noah's Ark Research Foundation Project, lecture by Allen S. Roberts, 1992.

The Remarkable Birth of Planet Earth (2nd Edition). Henry M. Morris. San Diego, CA: Creation Life Publisher, 1978.

Secrets: On the Ethics of Concealment and Revelation. New York, NY: Vintage Books, 1983.

"Six Flood Arguments Creationists Can't Answer." Robert J. Schadewald *Creation/Evolution,* Issue #9, 1982.

Where Is Noah's Ark? Lloyd R. Bailey. Nashville, TN: Abingdon Press, 1978.